SLOW COOKING FOR

BEGINNERS

The step-by-step guide to slow cooking with over 35 delicious slow cooking recipes for eating clean

Disclaimer

Contents

Introduction

At the end of a busy day, the last thing you want to do is spend hours in the kitchen. Skip all the work and dish up one of the slow cooking recipes shown here instead. This book covers a wide spectrum of dishes including pork roast, cabbage rolls, lamb stuffed yellow squash, sweet and sour meatballs and delicious salsa cheesecake. These quick and easy dinners are perfect for busy weeknights.

We have also covered an array of dishes, like tender duck in red curry, glazed chicken thighs, and rosemary pork buns. We've even got slow cooker dessert recipes like apple butter, chocolate cake and caramelized banana to please your sweet tooth.

Give your oven a break this holiday season, these recipes along with user-friendly cooking tips, health and diet information with nutrient analysis are easy to cook and is sure to be a welcome break for the whole house.

Try out the long-simmering soups and stews when the weather is cold outside. With a slow cooker you can have fantastic meals which you couldn't cook otherwise because of tight schedules.

These dishes are carefully handpicked to ensure a balance between tasty food and healthy eating. They keep in mind the busy schedules of today and ensure that you spend as little time as possible in preparation without compromising on the quality of the final dishes.

You can make delicious, healthy dishes for the whole family the "throw-'n'-go" way: Simply add ingredients to the cooker, get on with your day, and come home to a kitchen filled with mouth watering aromas.

This book is a perfect read for someone who has spent years with slow cooking but is looking for new dishes to add to their arsenal. At the same it can be used by someone who is new to the kitchen who has never heard of slow cooking before.

With clearly demarcated sections for nutritional information, ingredients and the cooking process itself, this book should be easy to follow even for non native English speakers. Wake up the chef in you and head over to the kitchen to whip up some mouth watering dishes that are sure to make your tummy purr with pleasure. You just can't stop with one serving!!

About Slow Cooking

Slow-cooking is a method of food preparation using low-heat for long hours. It is a process of cooking food in which all the connective tissues are broken down and the food becomes incredibly tender. Slow cooking makes the flavor infuse over long hours and provide deeper results than with virtually any other cooking method.

Slow cooking developed over a period of time when populations didn't have the financial resources to afford the tender cheap cuts of meat. They had to make do with whatever they could afford. To make them edible, they cooked them on a low heat over a long period of time. That is how it got its name 'slow cooking'.

The slow cooker is basically an electric pot with a stoneware insert. The cooking vessel could be oven, cast iron, ceramic pot, heated rock etc. It comes in a lot of sizes and range from 1 to 6 quarts. It is very convenient to use as it comes with only a few settings, such as 'high',' medium' and 'low'. It is better than oven or stovetop burner in a way that it can cook food at consistently low and even temperatures for what might be as long as 10 or 12 hours.

These units require minimal food preparation and are safe enough to turn on before work and return to before dinner, with fully-cooked hot food ready to go. The slow-cooker is geared towards 'one-pot' recipes.

Simply cut the ingredients in large chunks, throw in the slow cooker, add seasoning, liquid and forget. Lengthy cooking, direct heat from the pot, and steam created within the tightly covered container combine to prevent bacteria growth and make slow cooking a safe process for cooking foods. Slow cooker automatically shift to "warm" mode when the cooking is finished so that the meal is absolutely ready to be eaten the second you walk into the door.

Slow cooking is mostly used for tough less expensive cuts of meat that cannot be cooked to a satisfying tenderness using other methods. To achieve the required tenderness, it has to be cooked for a fairly long period of time. The tougher the cut of meat, the longer you have to cook. Meat starts to contract at temperatures past 100°F and will begin to release its juices once it reaches 160°F. Collagen starts to break down at around 160ºF so meat that is being stewed need to reach and maintain a temperature of at least 160ºF for 3 to 6 hours.

Slow cookers are a fabulous way to still get that great dinner you want without spending hours in the kitchen. It is ideal for people who work long hours. Just throw the ingredients into a slow cooker in the morning and have a nice hot home cooked meal when you come home.

With slow cooker you can cook all kind of dishes you can imagine including side dishes, desserts, breads. You don't have to watch over it the whole time. You can get a richly flavored meal at the end of an 8- or 10-hour slow simmer. These days time-saving is the foremost reason for the slow cooker's popularity. Dinner is ready while you are out.

Benefits of slow cooking:

1. **Nutritious, Delicious Meals**
   Slow cooking is done with fresh ingredients. The cooking retains the nutritious, natural juices from meats and vegetables.

2. **Save money**
   Slow cookers are great for cooking less expensive cuts like lamb shoulder, beef brisket, chicken thighs and pork shoulder.

3. **Multiple cooking**
   Slow cooking can be used for baking, poaching, roasting, braising. Thus this one pot meets multiple cooking needs.

4. **Time-saver**
   There is no more slaving in the kitchen for long hours. All that's required is the initial prep. Just throw all the ingredients in your slow-cooker and it will do all the work while you are doing whatever else you want or need to be doing. Prepare everything the night, place inside the slow-cooker and keep in the fridge overnight. Take it out of the fridge in the morning and leave for half an hour before turning the cooker on.

5. Leave your hands free

Slow cookers are designed to do their own cooking so you don't need to keep checking the contents. You can choose recipes where most of the ingredients can be added at the beginning. This will leave your hands free to do other things.

6. Useful Year-Round

The beauty of slow-cookers is that you can use them any time of year for cooking any type of food.

7. Versatile for all kinds of foods

The slow cooker is a versatile cooking appliance that is suitable to cook vegetarian foods as well as meat and poultry.

8. Thickening

The liquid doesn't reduce or thicken. You can either roll your meat in a small amount of seasoned flour at the beginning or you can mix a little cornflour with cold water to make a paste and stir into your simmering slow cooker contents at the end and then replace the lid.

9. Reduced Energy Usage

Slow-cookers use energy substantially less than a conventional electric oven.

10.   Easy Clean-Up

The best part is easy clean up. As it involves cooking in a single pot you don't need to clean up any other utensils except for a cutting board, knife and spoon.

11.   Transportable

Slow cooker is portable and slow-cooked meal can be easily transported from one place to another.

12.   Trim the fat

There's enough moisture in the slow cooker, therefore you don't need to add extra oil. Heath conscious people don't like much fat on their meat. One of the benefits of slow cooker is that you can always trim off fat.

13.   Go easy on the liquid

The liquid doesn't evaporate because of the tightly sealed lid, so it's best to reduce the amount of liquid. Add liquid just enough to cover the meat and vegetables. You don't need to overfill your slow cooker.

Safe slow cooking tips:

Before you get started, though, here's some slow cooking tips need to know to cook successfully:

1. Spraying the inside of the cooker with nonstick cooking spray before cooking make cleaning up easier and hassle free.
2. Slow cooking doesn't lose as much moisture as conventional cooking methods do. In spite of the fact that you may be enticed - don't add more water to the cooker than the recipe calls for.
3. Meats doesn't brown in the slow cooker, so you need to brown the meat in a skillet before placing it in the slow cooker for recipes requiring browned meat
4. Surprisingly vegetables take longer to cook than meat, so always put in vegetables first when you are cooking meat and vegetables together
5. Don't keep finished dishes in the slow cooker for too long. Foods need to be kept cooler than 40°F or hotter than 140°F to avoid harmful bacteria.
6. Do don't use your slow cooker for reheating leftovers. Use the microwave oven, range or oven for reheating.
7. Defrost meat or poultry completely before cooking in the slow cooker.

8. Always cut food into one-inch chunks or smaller pieces before cooking
9. Never cook a whole chicken inside the slow cooker, since the temperature inside a whole chicken doesn't reach a safe temperature quickly enough to prevent bacteria growth.
10. When doing advanced preparation, keep perishable foods refrigerated until preparation time.
11. Several factors affect cooking time- slow cooker's idiosyncrasies, amount of food is in the cooker, temperature of the ingredients and the humidity. Therefore cooking times in all recipes are approximations.
12. If the power goes out while you are out, check the temperature of the food with a thermometer. If it is below 165°F, discard it.

Appetizers

Island Pork Roast with Pineapple Chunks

Serves: 10

Time: 6 Hrs

Nutritional Information: Calories 342, Fat 7.5g, Protein 35.9g, Carbohydrates 26g, Fiber 1g

Ingredients

2 cans (8 ounces each) unsweetened pineapple chunks, undrained

1 boneless pork loin roast (about 4 pounds)

1/4 cup packed brown sugar

2 tablespoons teriyaki sauce

1 large onion, sliced

1/2 cup sugar

1/2 cup lime juice

1/2 cup soy sauce

1/4 teaspoon pepper

1 bay leaf

2 garlic cloves, minced

1 teaspoon ground ginger

1 teaspoon curry powder

1/4 cup cornstarch

1/4 teaspoon salt

Cooking Method

1. Drain pineapple and reserve its juice. Keep aside
2. Take 4-qt. slow cooker and place onion in it. Cut pork roast in half. And add to onion in the cooker.
3. Combine soy sauce sugar, lime juice, teriyaki sauce, brown sugar, curry, garlic, bay leaf, reserved pineapple juice, ginger, pepper and salt in a small bowl.
4. Pour this soy sauce mixture over pork. Cover the cooker.
5. Cook on low for 6 hours or until a meat thermometer reads 160°. Add pineapple pieces during the 6th hour and cook.
6. Take out the cooked meat with pineapple and onion and transfer to a serving platter.
7. Take out fat from cooking juices; transfer to a small pan. Bring to a boil.
8. In a small bowl mix cornstarch in water to form a smooth paste.
9. Pour this paste into the pan with fat.
10. Cook for a couple of minutes until the mixture is thickened.
11. Serve this cornstarch gravy over slow cooked pork.

Lamb Stuffed Yellow Squash

Serves: 4

Time: 6 Hrs

Nutritional Information: Calories 343, Fat 14.5g, Protein 14.7g, Carbohydrates 37.5g, Fiber 5g

Ingredients

8 ounces lean ground lamb

1/4 cup uncooked converted rice

8 medium yellow squash

4 teaspoons minced garlic, divided

3/4 teaspoon ground cinnamon

1/4 cup chopped fresh parsley

3/4 teaspoon ground allspice

1/2 teaspoon freshly ground black pepper

1/2 cup finely chopped onion

1 (14.5-ounce) can petite diced tomatoes, undrained

2 teaspoons brown sugar

1 (15-ounce) can no-salt-added tomato sauce

Cooking Method

1. Take 8 yellow fresh squash and slice off its narrow neck. Insert a small paring knife into squash. Carefully twist knife inside the squash and scoop out its pulp. Be careful not to pierce the sides of squash.
2. Combine 2 teaspoons garlic, parsley, salt, all spice, cinnamon and black pepper in a bowl. Add in lamb and uncooked rice into the mixture. Mix well
3. Take each hollow squash and stuff it with the lamb & rice mixture evenly.
4. Coat a 5-quart electric slow cooker with cooking spray. Place all the stuffed squash horizontally in the cooker.
5. Combine remaining brown sugar, 2 teaspoons garlic, onion, diced tomatoes and tomato sauce and pour over squash.
6. Cover and cook on LOW for next 6 hours. Squash will turn tender. Serve squash with sauce of your choice.

Turkey & Beans Chili

Serves: 6

Time: 4 Hrs

Nutritional Information: Calories 346, Fat 7.4g, Protein 26.g, Carbohydrates 48.3g, Fiber 11.4g

Ingredients

1 pound lean ground turkey

1-3/4 cups frozen corn, thawed

1 medium green pepper, finely chopped

1 can (15 ounces) black beans, rinsed and drained

1 small red onion, finely chopped

1 can (16 ounces) kidney beans, rinsed and drained

2 garlic cloves, minced

1 can (28 ounces) diced tomatoes, undrained

1 can (14-1/2 ounces) reduced-sodium chicken broth

1 tablespoon chili powder

1/4 teaspoon garlic powder

1/2 teaspoon pepper

1/4 teaspoon ground cumin

1 can (6 ounces) tomato paste

Cooking Method

1. In a large nonstick saucepan, sauté onion, garlic and green pepper for 2 minutes.
2. Add in turkey over medium heat and cook until meat is no longer pink. Drain.
3. Now transfer the meat along onion and pepper to a 4-qt. slow cooker.
4. Add in the black beans, corn, tomatoes, kidney beans, broth, tomato paste, cumin, chili powder, garlic powder and pepper.
5. Cover and cook on low for 4-5 hours.

Slow Cooked Gingered Ribs

Serves: 4

Time: 8 Hrs

Nutritional Information: Calories 598, Fat 23g, Protein 41g, Carbohydrates 53g, Fiber 9.5g

Ingredients

2 medium parsnips, peeled and halved

4 pounds bone-in beef short ribs

1 tablespoon minced fresh gingerroot

2 large carrots, halved

1/2 cup reduced-sodium soy sauce

1 small head cabbage, quartered

1/4 cup rice vinegar

2 garlic cloves, minced

1/3 cup packed brown sugar

1/2 teaspoon crushed red pepper flakes

2 tablespoons cornstarch

2 tablespoons cold water

2 teaspoons sesame oil

Cooking Method

1. Place the parsnips, carrots and ribs in a 5-qt. slow cooker.
2. Combine the brown sugar, soy sauce, pepper flakes, vinegar, garlic and ginger in a bowl; pour this mixture over ribs. Add in quartered cabbage.
3. Cover and cook on low for 7 hours or until meat is tender. Transfer cooked meat along with vegetables to a serving platter. Keep warm.
4. Remove fat from cooking juices and transfer this fat free juice to a small saucepan. Bring liquid to a boil.
5. Meanwhile combine cornstarch in water to form a smooth paste. Gradually stir into the boiling cooking juices. Cook and stir for 3 minutes or until the juice thickened.
6. Add in sesame oil. Pour this juicy sauce over meat and vegetables.
7. Serve with couscous and green onions if desired.

Rosemary Pork Buns with Horseradish Aioli

Serves: 12

Time: 8 Hrs

Nutritional Information: Calories 411, Fat 21.3g, Protein 25g, Carbohydrates 36g, Fiber 2.4g

Ingredients

1 (1 1/2-pound) boneless pork loin roast, trimmed

1/2 cup vertically sliced shallots (2 large)

1/2 teaspoon freshly ground black pepper

1 cup water

1 cup fat-free, lower-sodium chicken broth

24 (1.3-ounce) wheat buns, split

2 teaspoons prepared horseradish

1 tablespoon chopped fresh rosemary

4 garlic cloves, minced

3/4 cup canola mayonnaise

2 cups arugula

Cooking Method

1. Marinate pork loin with pepper. Heat a large skillet coated with cooking spray over medium-high heat.
2. Stir pork and cook both sides of the meat for 3 minutes until browned.
3. Transfer the meat to a 3-quart slow cooker. Add 1 cup water, chicken broth, shallots, rosemary and minced garlic to slow cooker.
4. Cover and cook on LOW for 8 hours or until tender. Place pork in a bowl and shred it with 2 forks. Strain cooking liquid from the cooker and reserve shallots and garlic.
5. Add only 3/4 cup of the cooking liquid, garlic and shallots to pork; toss well. Combine horseradish and mayonnaise in a small bowl.
6. Place a bun on a plate and spoon 2 tablespoons of pork mixture on the bun. Top with arugula and 1 teaspoons mayonnaise mixture. Cover with another bun.

Chicken Wing Drummettes with Blue Cheese Dip

Serves: 15

Time: 3 Hrs

Nutritional Information: Calories 94, Fat 4.7g, Protein 7.8g, Carbohydrates 4.3g, Fiber 0.6g

Ingredients

3 pounds chicken wing drummettes, skinned

1/4 teaspoon freshly ground black pepper

1 teaspoon reduced-sodium Worcestershire sauce

2 garlic cloves, minced

3/4 cup thick hot sauce

2 tablespoons cider vinegar

Cooking spray

30 carrot sticks

Blue Cheese Dip

30 celery sticks

Cooking Method

1. Preheat oven to 450°.
2. Line a jelly-roll pan with foil; coat this foil with cooking spray.
3. Marinate chicken with pepper and place it on pan. Spray cooking oil on chicken on pan
4. Bake, uncovered for 8-9 minutes.
5. Combine vinegar, hot sauce, Worcestershire sauce and garlic in an oval 4-quart electric slow cooker coated with cooking spray.
6. Take out browned chicken from oven; drain on paper towels.
7. Place chicken in slow cooker with other ingredients, mix gently to coat with sauce.
8. Cover and cook on HIGH for 3 hours.
9. Serve with Blue Cheese Dip, carrot sticks, and celery sticks.

Beef Chuck Roast with Alfredo Potatoes

Serves: 4

Time: 7.5 Hrs

Nutritional Information: Calories 123, Fat 4.6g, Protein 3.2g, Carbohydrates 22g, Fiber 2.3g

Ingredients

1 boneless beef chuck roast (4 pounds), trimmed

1 medium sweet red pepper, cut into 1-inch pieces

3/4 cup refrigerated Alfredo sauce

1 envelope brown gravy mix

1 cup chopped green pepper

8 medium red potatoes, quartered

1 envelope Italian salad dressing mix

2/3 cup chopped onion

2 tablespoons cornstarch

2 tablespoons butter

1/4 teaspoon pepper

1 tablespoon minced chives

Cooking Method

1. Cut beef chuck roast in half and place it in a 5-qt. slow cooker. Combine the dressing mix, gravy mix and water in a small bowl; pour this mix over meat.
2. Add in green pepper, red pepper and onion. Cover and cook on low for 6-8 hours or until meat is tender.
3. Bring potatoes in a large saucepan of water to a boil. Reduce heat; cover and simmer for 15 minutes or until tender.
4. While the potatoes are simmering, remove beef and cut one portion into small cubes, measuring 3 cups. Slice the remaining portion of the meat and keep warm. Skim fat from cooking juices. Pour the fat free cooking juices into a large skillet.
5. Combine cornstarch and cold water and make a smooth paste; stir this paste into cooking juices. Cook and stir for 2 minutes or until thickened.
6. Meanwhile drain the cooked potatoes; mash with butter, Alfredo sauce and pepper. Sprinkle with chives. Serve with sliced beef and gravy.

Glazed Chicken Thighs in Pineapple Juice

Serves: 6

Time: 3 Hrs

Nutritional Information: Calories 340, Fat 7.3g, Protein 31.9g, Carbohydrates 34.2g, Fiber 0.7g

Ingredients

1 cup pineapple juice

2 pounds skinless, boneless chicken thighs

2 tablespoons lower-sodium soy sauce

1/4 teaspoon salt

1 teaspoon olive oil

2 tablespoons light brown sugar

3 cups hot cooked rice

3 tablespoons water

2 tablespoons cornstarch

1/2 teaspoon freshly ground black pepper

Cooking Method

1. Marinate chicken with pepper and salt and keep aside for 5 minutes.
2. Heat oil in a large nonstick skillet over medium-high heat.
3. Add chicken thighs to pan. Cook for 5 minutes on each side or until browned.
4. Coat a 4-quart electric slow cooker coated with cooking spray and transfer browned chicken pieces to it.
5. Add in pineapple juice into drippings, stir and scrape bottom of the pan to loosen any browned bits.
6. Remove from heat; stir in soy sauce and brown sugar. Stir in pineapple juice mixture over chicken. Cover and cook on LOW for 2 1/2 hours.
7. Transfer chicken on a serving platter. Increase heat to HIGH and let the cooking juice simmer.
8. Combine cornstarch in 2 tablespoons of water in a small bowl; add this starch sauce in slow cooker, stirring with a wooden spoon.
9. Cook for 3 minutes or until sauce thickens, stirring constantly with spoon.
10. Place cooked rice on serving plates and top with chicken thighs and sauce.

Beef Stuffed Cabbage Rolls

Serves: 6

Time: 6 Hrs

Nutritional Information: Calories 206, Fat 8.7g, Protein 15.3g, Carbohydrates 14.3g, Fiber 0.8g

Ingredients

3/4 cup quick-cooking rice

1-1/2 pounds ground beef

1 large head cabbage

1 can (8 ounces) tomato sauce

1 egg, lightly beaten

1/2 cup chopped green pepper

1 can (46 ounces) V8 juice

1/2 cup crushed saltines (about 15 crackers)

1 ounce onion soup mix

Salt to taste

Grated Parmesan cheese

Cooking Method

1. Place whole cabbage inside boiling water and cook just until leaves fall off head.
2. Drain well and keep 10-12 large leaves aside which will be used for rolling.
3. Cut out the thick vein from the bottom of each reserved leaf, making a V-shaped cut; set aside.
4. Combine the rice, tomato sauce, egg and soup mix, green pepper and cracker crumbs in a large bowl. Add in crumbled beef and mix well.
5. Spread a cabbage leaf and place about 1/2 cup of the meat mixture on it.
6. Fold in sides, beginning from the cut end. Roll up completely to enclose filling and secure with toothpicks.
7. Make 12 cabbage rolls like this and put all the rolls inside a 3-qt. slow cooker. Pour V8 juice over rolls.
8. Cover and cook on low for 6-7 hours.
9. Sprinkle with salt and cheese before serving.

Pomegranate Red Jelly Glazed Ham

Serves: 12

Time: 7 Hrs

Nutritional Information: Calories 372, Fat 12g, Protein 48g, Carbohydrates 16g, Fiber 0.6g

Ingredients

1 cup pomegranate juice

1 small bone-in half ham (about 6 lb.)

2 tablespoons Dijon mustard

1/2 cup red currant jelly

1/4 cup packed dark brown sugar

Cooking Method

1. Put jelly in a nonstick saucepan over medium-low heat and cook for 4-5 minutes until softened; stirring continuously.
2. Pour the semi liquid jelly through a fine-mesh sieve into a bowl; discard any solid substance.
3. Cover and refrigerate for few hours.
4. Place ham and 1 cup pomegranate juice in a slow cooker; cover and cook for 5 hours on LOW; basting once or twice.
5. In a small saucepan, combine jelly, brown sugar, mustard and 3 tbsp. of cooking liquid from slow cooker.
6. Cook over high heat until sugar has dissolved; keep stirring
7. Discard 1 cup of cooking liquid from slow cooker.
8. Pour the mixture from saucepan over ham.
9. Cover cooker and increase heat to high.
10. Cook for half an hour, basting often, until shiny and glazed.
11. Place cooked ham to a serving platter and let stand at room temperature before serving

Corn and Potato Chowder with Bacon

Serves: 4

Time: 7 Hrs 20 Min

Nutritional Information: Calories 353, Fat 6.7g, Protein 9.6g, Carbohydrates 70g, Fiber 7g

Ingredients

6 slices bacon, sliced

2 cups potatoes, diced, peeled

16 ounces cream-style corn

1/2 cup onion, chopped

1 tablespoon sugar

20 ounces frozen whole kernel corn, broken apart

1 teaspoon seasoning salt

1 teaspoon Worcestershire sauce

1/4 teaspoon pepper

1 cup water

Cooking Method

1. Heat oil in a nonstick skillet over medium heat.
2. Add in bacon slice and fry both sides for 10 minutes until browned. Remove and keep aside.
3. Add onion and potatoes to bacon drippings and sauté' for about five minutes; drain well.
4. Combine all ingredients including browned bacon, onion, potatoes, corn, Worcestershire sauce, sugar, salt & pepper in slow cooker. Stir well.
5. Cover and cook on LOW setting for 6 - 7 hours.
6. Spoon corn chowder into serving plates

Spicy Slow Cooker Chickpeas

Serves: 6

Time: 8 Hrs 20 Min

Nutritional Information: Calories 268, Fat 4.3g, Protein 9.8 g, Carbohydrates 47g, Fiber 9.4g

Ingredients

2 (19 ounce) cans chickpeas, rinsed and drained

2 onions, peeled and finely chopped

4 garlic cloves, finely chopped

1 teaspoon cumin seed

1 teaspoon salt

1/2 teaspoon fresh ground black pepper

1/2 teaspoon cayenne pepper

2 teaspoons ground coriander

2 teaspoons balsamic vinegar

2 cups coarsely chopped tomatoes

2 tablespoons minced fresh gingerroot

1 tablespoon vegetable oil

Cooking Method

1. Heat oil in a nonstick skillet over medium heat. Add onions and sauté for 3 minutes just until they begin to brown.
2. Then add chopped garlic and cook for another one minute.
3. Then add gingerroot, coriander, cumin pepper, salt and cook, stirring, for 1 minute.
4. Add tomatoes and vinegar and bring to a boil.
5. Transfer this mixture into slow cooker; add chickpeas and combine well.
6. Cover and cook on Low for 6-7 hours until the mixture is hot and bubbling.
7. Serve with pita bread.

Cuban Beef & Pepper Stew

Serves: 8

Time: 8 Hrs

Nutritional Information: Calories 301, Fat 15.3g, Protein 26g, Carbohydrates 15.7g, Fiber 3.9g

Ingredients

3 cans (14-1/2 ounces each) diced tomatoes, undrained

2 tablespoons olive oil

2 large onions, coarsely chopped

4 jalapeno peppers, seeded and minced

2 large green peppers, coarsely chopped

1 habanero pepper, seeded and minced

2 pounds boneless beef roast, halved

6 garlic cloves, minced

2 tablespoons minced fresh cilantro

1/2 cup pimiento-stuffed olives, coarsely chopped

4 teaspoons beef bouillon granules

1 teaspoon dried oregano

2 teaspoons pepper

1-1/2 teaspoons ground cumin

Cooking Method

1. Heat oil a large nonstick saucepan over medium-high heat; place beef and cook until browned on both sides.
2. Transfer browned beef to a 5-qt. slow cooker. Add green pepper, jalapeno, onions and habanero.
3. Combine beef bouillon, tomatoes, oregano, water, cumin, garlic, pepper, and cilantro in a bowl. Pour this mixture over vegetables and beef.
4. Cover and cook on low for 8 hours till meat is soft & tender. Remove beef and let the cooking juices cool slightly.
5. Skim off fat from cooking juices. Shred beef with two forks and return to slow cooker. Add in olives and heat through. Serve with rice if desired.

Vegetable Pot Pie with Biscuits Toppings

Serves: 8

Time: 5 Hrs

Nutritional Information: Calories 342, Fat 11.4g, Protein 12g, Carbohydrates 43.6g, Fiber 5.6g

Ingredients

Filling:

2 cups frozen petite green peas

2 cups diced peeled baking potato (8 ounces)

1 1/4 cups diced carrot (3 carrots)

2 (8-ounce) packages sliced cremini mushrooms

1 cup diced parsnip (2 parsnips)

3/4 cup chopped celery (3 stalks)

1/2 teaspoon freshly ground black pepper

1/4 teaspoon salt

2 garlic cloves, minced

Cooking spray

1 (16-ounce) package frozen pearl onions

1 1/2 tablespoons chopped fresh thyme

2 1/2 tablespoons all-purpose flour

3/4 cup organic vegetable broth

2 tablespoons olive oil, divided

1 1/2 cups 1% low-fat milk

Biscuit topping:

2 ounces grated fresh Parmesan cheese (about 1/2 cup)

7.5 ounces all-purpose flour (about 1 2/3 cups)

3/4 teaspoon baking soda

1 1/2 teaspoons baking powder

1/8 teaspoon salt

1 teaspoon freshly ground black pepper

4 1/2 tablespoons unsalted butter, cut into pieces

1 cup low-fat buttermilk

3 tablespoons chopped fresh chives

Cooking Method

1. To make the filling, heat a large nonstick skillet coated with cooking oil over medium-high heat.
2. Add carrot, potato, parsnip, celery, mushrooms, salt and black pepper; cook for 5 minutes. Stir in minced garlic; sauté for 1 minute.
3. Transfer all the vegetables into a 5-quart electric slow cooker coated with cooking spray.
4. Heat 1 tablespoons oil in a skillet over medium-high heat. Add 2 1/2 tablespoons flour and cook for 1 minute. Keep stirring with a whisk.
5. Slowly add broth and milk, stirring continuously to avoid lump formation.
6. Cook for 4-5 minutes until the sauce is thickened, stirring constantly the whole time with a wooden spoon.
7. Pour this saucy mixture into the cooker. Add in thyme, peas and onions. Cover and cook on LOW for 3 1/2 hours or until vegetables are tender.
8. To make biscuit topping; whisk flour, baking soda, baking powder, salt and black pepper in a large bowl.
9. Cut in butter until mixture resembles coarse meal.
10. Add in buttermilk, chives and cheese; stirring just until moist.

11. Increase slow cooker heat to HIGH. Drop biscuits mixture onto filling in 8 equal mounds.
12. Cover and cook on HIGH for 1 hour and 15 minutes. Uncover and let stand for 6-7 minutes before serving.

Main Dishes

Slow-Simmered Bacon with Kidney Beans

Serves: 16

Time: 6 Hrs

Nutritional Information: Calories 213, Fat 9.6g, Protein 5.3g, Carbohydrates 31g, Fiber 3.1g

Ingredients

1/2 pound smoked Polish sausage

6 bacon strips, diced

2 medium sweet red peppers, chopped

4 cans (16 ounces each) kidney beans, rinsed and drained

1 can (28 ounces) diced tomatoes, drained

1/4 cup molasses

1 large onion, chopped

1 cup ketchup

1/2 cup packed brown sugar

2 medium unpeeled red apples, cubed

1/4 cup honey

1 teaspoon salt

1 teaspoon ground mustard

1 tablespoon Worcestershire sauce

Cooking Method

1. Cook bacon strips in a large skillet until cooked and crisp. Remove the cooked strips onto paper towels.
2. Add sausage to drippings; cook for 6 minutes. Drain and set aside.
3. Combine the red peppers, beans, tomatoes, brown sugar, onion, ketchup, mustard, honey, Worcestershire sauce, salt and molasses in a 5-qt. slow cooker.
4. Add in sausage and bacon strips. Cover and cook on low for 4 hours. Stir in apples.
5. Cover and cook for 2 more hours.

Lasagna Layered with Sausage and Cheese

Serves: 10

Time: 6 Hrs

Nutritional Information: Calories 633, Fat 34g, Protein 40.1g, Carbohydrates 45.6g, Fiber 3.9g

Ingredients

1 pound Italian Sausage

1 pound ground turkey

3/4 cup chopped sweet onion

1 can (28 ounces) crushed tomatoes, undrained

3 garlic cloves, minced

3 tablespoons dried parsley flakes, divided

3 cans (15 ounces each) tomato sauce

1/3 cup sugar

2 teaspoons dried basil

1/4 cup dry red wine

3 teaspoons dried oregano, divided

1/2 teaspoon salt, divided

2-1/2 cups ricotta cheese

1 cup grated Parmesan cheese

3 cups (12 ounces) shredded mozzarella cheese

1 package (9 ounces) no-cook lasagna noodles

Cooking Method

1. Place a Dutch oven over medium heat; add sausage, turkey, garlic and cook until sausage and turkey is no longer pink; drain.
2. Add in the crushed tomatoes, 2 tbs. Oregano, tomato sauce, 2 tbs. parsley, sugar, basil and 1/4 teaspoon salt to the meat.
3. Bring to a boil first and then reduce the heat. Let it simmer, uncovered, for 40 minutes.
4. Add in red wine and cook for 16 more minutes.
5. In a large bowl, combine ricotta cheese, parmesan cheese and mozzarella cheese. Add in oregano, parsley and salt.
6. Spread two cups of meat mixture in the bottom of a 6-qt. slow cooker. Arrange five noodles over sauce.
7. Spread 1 cup of the cheese mixture over noodles. Repeat layers twice. Spread remaining meat mixture on the top.
8. Cover and cook on low for 5 hours or until noodles are tender.

Sweet and Sour Jelly Meatballs

Serves: 10

Time: 4 Hrs

Nutritional Information: Calories 301, Fat 0.4g, Protein 2.2 g, Carbohydrates 76g, Fiber 4g

Ingredients

1 (14 ounce) jar chili sauce (like Heinz)

1 (15 ounce) can tomato sauce

1 (32 ounce) jar grape jelly

1 (7 ounce) can chopped mild green chilies

3 tablespoons dried onion flakes

1 tablespoon garlic powder

1 teaspoon of your favorite curry powder, to taste

1/2 teaspoon dried ancho chile powder

1/4 teaspoon dried chipotle powder, to taste

2 lbs pre-cooked frozen meatballs

Cooking Method

1. Mix all the ingredients chillies, onion flakes, garlic powder, curry powder, ancho chile powder, chipotle powder in a large bowl.
2. Now add chili sauce, tomato sauce and grape jelly to it and mix well
3. Transfer this mixture into slow cooker.
4. Add the meatballs and stir to coat well.
5. Cover and cook on low for 4 hours.
6. If you are using use thawed meatballs, it'll only less time in the slow cooker.
7. Serve these meatballs topped with sweet and sour sauce.

Sparerib, Bacon & Sauerkraut Supper

Serves: 4

Time: 7 Hrs

Nutritional Information: Calories 743, Fat 33g, Protein 58.9g, Carbohydrates 34.8g, Fiber 1.4g

Ingredients

2 pounds pork spareribs

3 slices thick-sliced bacon strips, cooked and crumbled

1 pound fingerling potatoes

1 medium onion, chopped

1/2 pound smoked Polish sausage, cut into 1-inch slices

1 jar (16 ounces) sauerkraut, undrained

1 medium apple, peeled and chopped

1/4 teaspoon caraway seeds

3 tablespoons brown sugar

1/2 teaspoon salt

1/4 teaspoon pepper

1 tablespoon vegetable oil

1 cup beer

Cooking Method

1. Drain sauerkraut and reserve 1/3 cup of the liquid
2. Place onion, potatoes, bacon and apple in a 6-qt. slow cooker.
3. Add in sauerkraut and reserved liquid to bacon.
4. Cut pork into serving-size portions; marinate with salt and pepper. In a large non-stick saucepan, heat oil over medium-high heat; cook ribs until browned in batches.
5. Transfer all the ingredients to slow cooker; stir in caraway seeds and brown sugar.
6. Add sausage and 1 cup beer.
7. Cover and cook on low for 6-7 hours. Allow the mixture to cool before serving

Salsa Cheesecake

Serves: 20

Time: 2 Hrs

Nutritional Information: Calories 59, Fat 2.6g, Protein 4,5g, Carbohydrates 3.3g, Fiber 0.4g

Ingredients

1 (8-ounce) tub fat-free cream cheese, softened

1 (8-ounce) tub light cream cheese with onions and chives

1/2 cup reduced fat 4-cheese Mexican blend cheese

Cooking spray

1 tablespoon dry breadcrumbs

1/2 cup bottled medium salsa

1 large egg white

1 large egg

1 tablespoon all-purpose flour

2 teaspoons chili powder

1/4 cup chopped seeded tomato

3 tablespoons sliced green onions

1 teaspoon ground cumin

1 (4.5-ounce) can chopped green chilies, undrained

4 cups hot water

3 tbs. yellow bell pepper, chopped

1/4 cup chopped fresh cilantro

Cooking Method

1. Sprinkle breadcrumbs over bottom of a 7-inch springform pan coated with cooking spray.
2. Wrap bottom and sides of the pan with foil.
3. Beat fat free and light cream cheese in a mixer until smooth at medium speed.
4. Add all purpose flour, salsa, chili powder, cumin and green chilies); beat until everything is blended.
5. Beat egg and egg white with a whisk in bowl. Add this to flour mixture.
6. Add in Mexican blend cheese. Pour this egg & cheese mixture into springform pan.
7. Take a 5-quart electric slow cooker and place a 10-ounce custard cup or ramekin, upside down inside the cooker.
8. Pour 4 cups hot water into slow cooker and place prepared pan on top of the custard cup.
9. Place 5-6 paper towels over top of cooker. Cover and cook on HIGH for 2 hours.
10. When cheesecake is set; discard paper towels (do not remove pan from crockery insert).
11. Run a sharp knife around cheesecake's edges. Take out crockery insert from cooker.
12. Let the cake stand, uncovered, in crockery insert for half an hour.
13. Remove springform pan from crockery insert, and let the cake cool completely. Cover and refrigerate for 24 hours.

14. Carefully remove sides from springform pan.
15. Layer tomato, cilantro, yellow bell pepper and green onions in the center of cheesecake.

Sweet & Tangy Collard Greens

Serves: 5

Time: 4 Hrs

Nutritional Information: Calories 81, Fat 1.6g, Protein 5.3g, Carbohydrates 12.1g, Fiber 3.9g

Ingredients

1 (16-ounce) package chopped fresh collard greens

3 bacon slices

2 garlic cloves, minced

1 cup chopped onion

1/4 teaspoon salt

1 bay leaf

1 tablespoon honey

1 (14.5-ounce) can fat-free, lower-sodium chicken broth

3 tablespoons balsamic vinegar

Cooking Method

1. Place bacon slices in a large slow cooker and cook over medium heat until crisp. Remove bacon from pan and crumble.
2. Add onion to drippings in a saucepan; sauté for 6 minutes.
3. Stir in collard greens, and cook for a couple of minutes until greens begin to wilt.
4. Transfer collard green mixture, minced garlic, bay leaf, chicken broth and salt in a 3-quart electric slow cooker.
5. Cover and cook on LOW for 3-4 hours.
6. Discard bay leaf.
7. Combine honey and vinegar in a small bowl; add into greens just before serving. Serve with bacon strips.

Mushrooms and Spinach Lasagna

Serves: 8

Time: 5 Hrs

Nutritional Information: Calories 397, Fat 17.3g, Protein 21.2g, Carbohydrates 37.5g, Fiber 2.3g

Ingredients

2 cups sliced cremini mushrooms

1 large egg, lightly beaten

4 cups torn spinach

1/2 cup commercial pesto

3/4 cup (3 ounces) shredded part-skim mozzarella cheese

3/4 cup (3 ounces) grated fresh Parmesan cheese, divided

3/4 cup (3 ounces) shredded provolone cheese

1 (15-ounce) carton fat-free ricotta cheese

1 (8-ounce) can tomato sauce

1 (25.5-ounce) bottle fat-free tomato-basil pasta sauce

Cooking spray

1 (8-ounce) package precooked lasagna noodles (12 noodles)

Cooking Method

1. Steam spinaches in a steamer for 2 minutes until spinach wilts. Drain completely and chop the spinaches coarsely.
2. In a large bowl; combine chopped spinach, pesto and mushrooms. Set aside.
3. Beat egg lightly in a bowl. Add in provolone and mozzarella; combine all the ingredients well.
4. Add in ricotta and one-fourth cup Parmesan; keep aside.
5. Combine tomato sauce and pasta sauce in a medium bowl.
6. Coat a 6-quart oval electric slow cooker with cooking spray.
7. Spread 1 cup of the pasta sauce mixture in the bottom of the cooker
8. Arrange 3 noodles over pasta sauce mixture; spread 1 cup cheese mixture over noodles and then top with 1 cup spinach mixture.
9. Make one more layer of pasta sauce, noodles, cheese and spinach mixture.
10. Now arrange 3 noodles over spinach; top with 1 cup cheese mixture and 1 cup pasta sauce mixture.
11. Place remaining 3 noodles over sauce mixture; spread remaining sauce mixture over noodles.
12. Add in the remaining 1/2 cup Parmesan.
13. Cover and cook on LOW for 5 hours.

Butternut Squash Soup

Serves: 8

Time: 6 Hrs

Nutritional Information: Calories 131, Fat 1.5g, Protein 3.6g, Carbohydrates 29g, Fiber 3g

Ingredients

3 (12-ounce) packages thawed butternut squash

2 cups chopped sweet onion (1 large)

1 1/2 cups chopped peeled apple (about 1 large)

2 cups chopped parsnip (3 large)

2 cups fat-free, lower-sodium chicken broth

1/4 teaspoon salt

1 teaspoon freshly ground black pepper

3 cups water

1/8 teaspoon paprika

1/8 teaspoon ground cumin

2 tablespoons whipping cream

8 teaspoons chopped fresh chives

1/2 cup light sour cream

Cooking Method

1. Combine sweet onion, parsnip, apple, squash, broth, pepper, salt and water in a 5-quart electric slow cooker. Cover and cook on LOW for 6 hours.
2. Remove center piece of blender lid to allow steam to escape.
3. Transfer 1/4 of squash mixture into a blender. Secure blender lid on blender. Place a clean towel over opening in blender lid and blend until smooth. Repeat with remaining squash.
4. Pour the blended mixture into a large bowl. Add in paprika, cumin and whipping cream into the soup.
5. Serve soup into bowls; top with chives and sour cream.

Veal and Leek Ragout

Serves: 8

Time: 5 Hrs

Nutritional Information: Calories 452, Fat 5g, Protein 39g, Carbohydrates 54g, Fiber 4.5g

Ingredients

3 cups sliced leek

1 (2 1/2-pound) boneless trimmed veal roast

3 cups (1/2-inch) slices peeled carrot

1/3 cup all-purpose flour

1 1/2 teaspoons paprika

3/4 teaspoon freshly ground black pepper

1 (14 1/2-ounce) can chicken broth

1/2 cup dry white wine

1/2 teaspoon salt

1 tablespoon olive oil, divided

3 garlic cloves, minced

5 thyme sprigs

1 bay leaf

2 tablespoons chopped fresh flat-leaf parsley

8 cups hot cooked fettuccine (about 16 ounces uncooked pasta)

Cooking Method

1. Cut 1-inch cubes of veal. Sprinkle with pepper, paprika and salt over veal.
2. Heat a large nonstick saucepan over medium-high heat. Add 1 teaspoon of cooking oil and swirl to coat.
3. Place half of veal into the pan; sauté for 5 minutes or until browned. Repeat the process with another half of the veal.
4. Transfer browned veal in a 6-quart electric slow cooker.
5. Add white wine to saucepan; cook for 1 minute and scrape the bottom of the pan to loosen browned bits. Pour this over already browned veal in slow cooker.
6. Heat 1 teaspoon of oil in skillet over medium-high heat.
7. Add garlic and sauté for 1 minute; add leek and cook for 3 minutes. Spoon this leek & garlic mixture over veal in slow cooker.
8. Blend flour and broth in a small bowl.
9. Pour broth mixture into slow cooker. Add thyme sprigs, bay leaf and carrot; stir well.
10. Cover and cook on LOW for 4 hours.
11. Discard thyme sprigs and bay leaf when veal looks tender.
12. Serve veal mixture over fettucine; sprinkle with parsley.

Chicken Stew with Olives over Couscous

Serves: 4

Time: 4 Hrs

Nutritional Information: Calories 438, Fat 15.6g, Protein 43g, Carbohydrates 31g, Fiber 4.3g

Ingredients

1 1/2 cups fat-free, lower-sodium chicken broth, divided

1 (3-pound) quartered chicken, skinned

2 (14.5-ounce) cans no-salt-added diced tomatoes, drained

1 onion, sliced

1/2 cup pitted green olives

1 garlic clove, minced

1/2 teaspoon turmeric

1 teaspoon ground cumin

Grated peel of 1 lemon

1 teaspoon paprika

Cooking spray

1/2 teaspoon freshly ground black pepper

2 cups hot cooked couscous

Cooking Method

1. Place tomatoes, onion, clove, cumin, paprika, turmeric and 1 cup broth in an electric slow cooker. Sprinkle chicken with pepper, lemon and salt.
2. Heat a large skillet coated with cooking spray over medium-high heat.
3. Add seasoned chicken to skillet; cook chicken for 6 minutes or until browned on both sides. Transfer browned chicken into slow cooker.
4. Add remaining half cup chicken broth into pan; scrape the bottom of pan to loosen browned bits. Pour this liquid over chicken inside slow cooker.
5. Cover and cook on HIGH for 3 1/2 hour. Stir in olives and cook for another half hour.
6. Remove chicken from slow cooker; cool. Separate meat from bones; discard bones and return meat to slow cooker. Serve chicken stew over couscous.

Steak Stroganoff with Mushrooms

Serves: 4

Time: 7 Hrs

Nutritional Information: Calories 453, Fat 15.6, Protein 35.4, Carbohydrates 40.3, Fiber 2.7g

Ingredients

1 (8-ounce) package sliced mushrooms (about 2 cups)

1 (1-pound) top round steak (1 inch thick), trimmed

1/2 teaspoon dried dill

1 cup chopped onion

1.5 ounces all-purpose flour (about 1/3 cup)

2 tablespoons chopped fresh parsley

1/2 teaspoon freshly ground black pepper

2 tablespoons Dijon mustard

1/2 teaspoon salt

3 garlic cloves, minced

1 cup fat-free, lower-sodium beef broth

1 (8-ounce) container low-fat sour cream

2 cups hot cooked medium egg noodles (about 4 ounces uncooked)

Cooking Method

1. Cut steak diagonally into 1/4-inch-thick slices.
2. Place steak, onion, parsley, Dijon, dill, salt, pepper, mushrooms and garlic in a 3-quart electric slow cooker; stir well.
3. Measure 1/3 cup of flour in a small bowl, add in broth and blend well with a whisk
4. Add flour & broth mixture to slow cooker; stir well. Cover and cook on HIGH for 1 hour.
5. Now cook on Low for 7 to 8 hours. Let stroganoff cool for 10 minutes. Add in sour cream. Serve stroganoff over noodles.

Eggplant Parmesan in Marinara Sauce

Serves: 6

Time: 7 Hrs

Nutritional Information: Calories 342, Fat 7g, Protein 20g, Carbohydrates 36g, Fiber 8g

Ingredients

2 large eggplants peeled and sliced into 1/3-inch rounds

1/4 cup chopped fresh basil

1 1/4 cups marinara sauce

3 large eggs

2 cups shredded mozzarella cheese

1 1/2 cups seasoned bread crumbs

Salt

Cooking Method

1. Sprinkle salt on both sides of the eggplant; place on paper towels, and let stand for fifteen minutes. Rinse; blot dry.
2. Coat inside of slow cooker with cooking spray. Spread 1/4 cup marinara sauce at the bottom of the cooker.
3. Beat eggs lightly
4. Dip eggplant in egg and then roll in bread crumbs.
5. Arrange a layer of dipped eggplant over marinara sauce. Spread with 1/4 cup sauce again; sprinkle with 1/2 cup cheese.
6. Make 4-5 layers of sauce, eggplant and cheese filling 2/3 portion of the cooker.
7. Cover and cook for 4-6 hours on low until eggplant is soft and mozzarella has melted.
8. Take out eggplants on serving plates, sprinkle with basil and serve.

Chili Cheese Pie with Cornmeal Crust

Serves: 8

Time: 6 Hrs

Nutritional Information: Calories 481, Fat 24g, Protein 28g, Carbohydrates 42g, Fiber 5g

Ingredients

1 1/2 pounds ground turkey

3/4 cup all-purpose flour

1 large onion, chopped

2 cloves garlic, minced

1 28-oz. can crushed tomatoes with liquid

2 tablespoons chili powder

1 cup low-sodium beef broth

3/4 cup yellow cornmeal

1 large egg, beaten

1 15-oz. can kidney beans, drained and rinsed

2 teaspoons baking powder

3/4 cup milk

1 cup grated Cheddar

1/4 cup vegetable oil

Cooking Method

1. Heat 2 tbsp. oil in a large skillet over medium-high heat. Add onion to skillet and sauté until softened. Add in garlic and chili powder and sauté for another 1 minute until fragrant.
2. Add in turkey, tomatoes and broth; mix well and break up any large piece of turkey. Add beans, bring to a boil. Transfer the meat and vegetable mixture into slow cooker coated with cooking spray.
3. Combine cornmeal, flour, salt and baking powder in a large bowl. Add in 1/4 cup oil, beaten egg, milk and cheese.
4. Pour the batter over turkey chili in slow cooker and gently spread to cover. Cover slow cooker and cook on low for 5 hours until chili is cooked through.

Tender Duck in Pineapple Red Curry

Serves: 6

Time: 2 ½ Hrs

Nutritional Information: Calories 658, Fat 49g, Protein 38g, Carbohydrates 20g, Fiber 2g

Ingredients

1 small pineapple, peeled, cored and cut into chunks

6 duck legs

2 tbsp fish sauce

2 tbsp light brown sugar

6 lime leaves

4 tbsp red Thai curry paste

1 can coconut milk

1 red chilli, deseeded and finely sliced, to serve

Thai basil leaves, to serve

Cooking Method

1. Heat oven to 180C/160C fan/gas 4. Fry both sides of duck legs in ovenproof frying pan on a low heat for 10 minutes. Remove legs from pan. Add some sugar to the fat left in the pan and let it caramelise. Stir in curry paste and sauté for a couple of minutes.
2. Add in the coconut milk and water. Combine everything and let it simmer, then add the fish sauce and lime leaves.
3. Add in the fried duck legs, cover the pan and cook in the oven for one and a half hour until the meat is really tender.
4. Transfer the legs into a serving dish and remove fat from the sauce. Refrigerate the curry for a couple of hours; it will be easier to remove the fat.
5. Add pineapple chunks to the pan over medium heat and let it simmer for 4 minutes. Add fish sauce and sugar according to your taste. Pour this curry over the duck; sprinkle with chilli and basil leaves.
6. Serve with jasmine rice.

Vegetable Bake with Aubergines & Courgettes

Serves: 6

Time: 6 Hrs

Nutritional Information: Calories 274, Fat 10g, Protein 14g, Carbohydrates 31g, Fiber 4g

Ingredients

300g/11oz baby or normal aubergines, sliced

4 garlic cloves, 3 crushed, 1 left whole

½ large jar roasted red peppers

400g can tomatoes, chopped

Oregano, chopped

Chilli flakes

2 courgettes, sliced

3 beef tomatoes, sliced

Basil leaves

Small baguette, sliced and toasted

2 x 125g balls mozzarella, torn

Green salad

Cooking Method

1. Chop all the vegetables according to directions. Divide the vegetables into two halves. Rub bread with garlic clove
2. Place slow cooker on High. Add in the canned tomatoes, half of the oregano leaves, crushed garlic, chilli and some seasoning. Cover and cook for 10 minutes.
3. Tip out most of the sauce. Layer up the vegetables and herbs with seasoning – the aubergines, courgettes, red peppers, tomatoes, basil and oregano.
4. Layer in the bread, mozzarella and half the tipped-out tomato sauce.
5. Repeat layers of vegetable, herb and tomato sauce layers, followed by the bread and mozzarella.
6. Cook on HIGH for 5 hrs. Flash under the grill before serving until golden and bubbling. Serve with a big salad on the side.

Chicken Casserole with Herby Dumplings

Serves: 6

Time: 2 ½ Hrs

Nutritional Information: Calories 701, Fat 37g, Protein 47g, Carbohydrates 38g, Fiber 3g

Ingredients

200g smoked bacon lardons

6 part-boned chicken breasts

300g large flat mushrooms, sliced

3 tbsp plain flour

3 tbsp olive oil

3 onions, each peeled and cut into 8 wedges

3 strips of peeled orange zest

3 garlic cloves, peeled and sliced

2 bay leaves

300ml red wine

300ml chicken stock

2 tbsp redcurrant sauce

For the dumplings

100g fresh white breadcrumbs

140g butter, cubed

2 tsp fresh thyme leaves, plus extra to serve

100g self-raising flour

2 tbsp fresh parsley, chopped

2 medium eggs, lightly beaten

1 tbsp wholegrain mustard

Cooking Method

1. Preheat the oven to fan 180C/ conventional 200C/gas 6.
2. Marinate chicken with salt and black pepper, coat gently with the flour. Heat the oil in ovenproof frying pan over high heat. Brown chicken on both sides in batches. Keep aside.
3. Add onions and lardons inside the same pan over low heat and cook for a couple of minutes until golden tinged.
4. Stir in garlic, then add the plain flour and cook for 2 minute, stirring continuously.
5. Stir in mushrooms, orange zest, redcurrant sauce and bay leaves. Cook about 5 minutes; then add the red wine and stock. Season with salt and pepper.
6. Bring to the boil, and then add the browned chicken to the pan, it should be well covered with the liquid. Cover and cook in the oven for 30 minutes.
7. To prepare the dumplings; put the flour, butter, mustard and breadcrumbs in a food processor and blitz.
8. Add in eggs, parsley, thyme, salt and pepper. Blitz until the mixture form moist dough. Put some flour on your hands and make 6 large even-sized balls.
9. Remove the casserole from the oven and place the dumplings on top. Cover and return to the oven for twenty minutes, until the casserole and dumplings is thoroughly cooked.

10. Spoon the chicken and sauce on six serving platters and top each with a dumpling. Serve with red wine.

Cottage Pie

Serves: 8

Time: 3 Hrs

Nutritional Information: Calories 600, Fat 32.3g, Protein 36.4g, Carbohydrates 41g, Fiber 4.1g

Ingredients

1¼kg beef mince

1large glass red wine

2 onions, finely chopped

3 carrots, chopped

2 garlic cloves, finely chopped

3 celery sticks, chopped

3 tbsp plain flour

3 tbsp olive oil

Thyme sprigs

1 tbsp tomato purée

2 bay leaves

850ml beef stock

4 tbsp Worcestershire sauce

For the mash

1.8kg potatoes, chopped

200g strong cheddar, grated

25g butter

Freshly grated nutmeg

225ml milk

Cooking Method

1. In a large saucepan, put potatoes in cold water with a pinch of salt, bring to the boil and let simmer until potato is tender.
2. Drain well and let it cool
3. Take 1 tbsp of oil in a large skillet and fry beef mince for a couple of minutes until browned. Keep it aside.
4. Heat oil in the pan over medium heat; cook the vegetables and about 20 minutes until soft.
5. Stir in garlic, flour and sauté for 5 minutes.
6. Add in tomato purée, and cook for a few minutes over high heat, then return the browned beef to the pan.
7. Add in red wine and bring to a boil to. Add in the herbs, stock, and Worcestershire sauce.
8. Let the mixture simmer for 45 minutes until the gray thickens.
9. Season well and then discard the thyme stalks and bay leaves.
10. Take the cooked potatoes and mash well.
11. Add in butter, milk, nutmeg, cheese, pepper and salt to taste. Mix everything well with the mashed potatoes.
12. Place meat mixture into an ovenproof dish.
13. Spoon on the potato mash over meat. Sprinkle with cheese if desired.
14. Heat oven to 220C/200C fan/gas 7 and cook for 30 minutes.
15. Serve immediately.

Chocolate Cake with Marshmallows

Serves:

Time: 4 Hrs 15 Min

Nutritional Information: Calories 715, Fat 34.3g, Protein 10g, Carbohydrates 89g, Fiber 4.3g

Ingredients

1 (4 ounce) package instant chocolate pudding mix

1 (18 1/4 ounce) package German chocolate cake mix

3 large eggs, lightly beaten

1/3 cup butter, melted

1 cup sour cream

1 teaspoon vanilla extract

1 (3 1/2 ounce) package chocolate cook-and-serve pudding mix

1/2 cup chopped pecans

3 1/4 cups milk, divided

1 cup semisweet chocolate morsel

1 1/2 cups miniature marshmallows

Cooking Method

1. To make batter, beat cake mix along with chocolate pudding mix in a bowl. Whisk eggs, sour cream, melted butter and vanilla extract together and add this mix to cake mix. Add 1 1/4 cups milk and run the batter in an electric mixer at medium speed for 2 minutes. Pour this batter gently into a lightly greased slow cooker.
2. Cook 2 cups milk in a nonstick saucepan over medium heat for 3-4 minutes just until bubbles appear. Note that you don't have to boil the milk.
3. Sprinkle cook-and-serve pudding mix over cake batter. Pour in hot milk over it. Cover and cook on LOW for 3 hours.
4. Heat pecans in a small pan over low heat until lightly toasted and fragrant. Sprinkle chocolate cake with chocolate morsels, pecans and marshmallows. Wait for marshmallows to melt.
5. Serve into dessert dishes with a topping of ice cream.

Tropical Fruit Cobbler

Serves: 6

Time: 4 Hrs 35 Min

Nutritional Information: Calories 387, Fat 13 g, Protein 5.7g, Carbohydrates 63g, Fiber 3.2 g

Ingredients

DOUGH

1 1/2 cups flour

2 tablespoons orange marmalade

2 teaspoons baking powder

1 tablespoon sugar

1 tablespoon shortening

4 tablespoons water

FILLING

1 cup pineapple tidbits

4 ounces cream cheese

2 cups gala apples, diced small

1/3 cup coconut

2 tablespoons sugar

SAUCE

2 cups apple cider

1/2 cup sugar

3 tablespoons flour

Cooking Method

Dough:

1. Combine together the flour with sugar and baking powder in a bowl.
2. Cut in the shortening until the mixture is crumbly.
3. Add in the marmalade. Add in water 1 tbsp at a time to make dough.
4. Place a moisten paper towel on the dough and set aside.

Filling:

5. Microwave the cream cheese for ten seconds until it turns soft
6. Combine together pineapple, coconut, apple and sugar in another medium bowl.

Sauce:

7. Pour the cider in a bowl. Add sugar to it and mix to dissolve the sugar
8. Sprinkle the flour into the crackpot. Pour the apple cider with dissolved sugar over the flour and stir to make sauce.

Assembly:

1. Divide the dough into 4 equal pieces and roll out to make each piece 1/4 inch thick.
2. Put 1/4 of the pineapple and coconut mixture into the center of the dough and fold over in the form of a half circle. Seal the edges.
3. Place all the four pastries in the slow cooker
4. Pour the cider/sugar mixture over the pastries.
5. Put the lid on the slow cooker and cook for 4 hours.
6. The dough will puff up a little and break open to make it look like a cobbler.

Bread Pudding with Dutch Honey Syrup

Serves: 12

Time: 1 Hrs 15 Min

Nutritional Information: Calories 237, Fat 11g, Protein 6.7g, Carbohydrates 28.5g, Fiber 1.2g

Ingredients

1 loaf whole wheat bread

3 -3 1/2 cups milk

6 eggs

1 (15 ounce) can pumpkin

1 cup brown sugar

2 teaspoons pure vanilla extract

1 teaspoon cinnamon

1/4 teaspoon cardamom

1/2 teaspoon ginger

1/2-1 cup raisins

1/2 teaspoon nutmeg

1 -2 cup chopped walnuts

Cooking Method

1. Place the bread crumbs in a large bowl.
2. Beat the eggs in a bowl. Add in 3 cups milk, pumpkin, spices and sugar in the bowl and mix well.
3. Pour this mixture into bowl of bread crumbs. Let the bread soak up the milk and add more milk if it looks dry. Add nuts and raisins.
4. Transfer this bread crumb mixture into large casserole dish. It needs 1-2 inches of head space. Add milk if needed to fill holes.
5. Cover with a foil and cook in a slow cooker on Low for 4-6 hours. Check with a skewer.
6. While it is cooking make the Dutch Honey (Dutch Honey Syrup).

Caramelized Banana Cake

Serves: 6

Time: 3Hrs 40 Min

Nutritional Information: Calories 564.3, Fat 18.7g, Protein 4.7g, Carbohydrates 97g, Fiber 4.5g

Ingredients

Banana

6 ripe medium bananas

6 tablespoons unsalted butter

1 cup dark brown sugar

3 tablespoons dark rum

Cake

3/4 cup cake flour

1 1/4 teaspoons ground nutmeg

2/3 cup sugar

1 1/4 teaspoons fine salt

1 1/2 teaspoons ground cinnamon

4 tablespoons unsalted butter

1 large egg, at room temperature

3/4 teaspoon baking powder

1 large egg yolk, at room temperature

2 tablespoons whole milk, at room temperature

Ice cream, for serving

Cooking Method

1. Coat the inside of a slow cooker with butter, line with a foil and then butter the foil. Turn the heat to HIGH.
2. Coat the bottom of the slow cooker well with more butter, brown sugar and rum over the foil.
3. Pee the bananas and cut them into halves along its length. Cover the bottom of the cooker with banana halves, cut side down. Press the bananas gently.
4. To make cake batter; combine the flour, cinnamon nutmeg, baking powder and salt in a large bowl.
5. Soften butter in a microwave for 10 seconds.
6. Blend butter and sugar in a bowl with an electric mixer at a medium speed. Gently raise speed to high and beat until the moisture turns light. Scrape the sides of the bowl occasionally.
7. Beat in the egg and then the yolk.
8. Add the butter and milk the flour mixture. Mix smoothly to make a smooth batter at medium speed.
9. Pour this batter over the bananas in the cooker and spread it evenly with a spatula.
10. Cover the top of the slow cooker from end to end with a large paper towel to create a tight seal.
11. Cover with the lid and cook on HIGH about 3 ½ hours, until the cake begins to brown slightly on the sides.

12. Keep the cake aside for 20 minutes or more after turning off the slow cooker.
13. Lift the whole cake along with the foil from inside the slow cooker; keep it on the counter to cool for half an hour or more.
14. Carefully invert the caramelized banana cake onto a plate.
15. Spoon cake into bowls and serve with ice cream, if desired.

All Day Apple Butter

Serves: 3

Time: 8-10 Hrs

Nutritional Information: Calories 1300, Fat 1.9g, Protein 2.8g, Carbohydrates 343g, Fiber 26g

Ingredients

5 lbs Granny smith apples, peeled and finely sliced

2 teaspoons ground cinnamon

3 cups sugar

1/4 teaspoon ground cloves

1/4 teaspoon salt

1/2 teaspoon allspice

1/4 teaspoon ground nutmeg

Grated rind and juice of 1 lemon

Cooking Method

1. Put apples in slow cooker in three layers, placing sugar between each layer.
2. Mix cinnamon, cloves, nutmeg, all spice, lemon rind and salt in a bowl.
3. Add this mixture on top and pack them down as well as you can.
4. Cover and cook on high for 1 hour.
5. Reduce heat to low. Open and stir it once.
6. Keep covered and cook for another 8 hours or until thick and dark brown, stirring occasionally.
7. Uncover and cook for the last hour on low.
8. For smoother apple butter, you may puree in a food mill.
9. Sterile jars for 10 minutes in hot water for canning.
10. Pour the apple butter into hot sterilized jars.

Conclusion

Whether you're busy at work or with the kids all day, there's nothing better than coming home to a ready-made, comforting meal that's ready to be eaten right away. Slow-cookers are a great complement to suit busy lifestyles. Throw the ingredients in the crock pot and let the meal cooks itself.

This book brings together a variety of recipes that show off the value, ease, delicious taste and versatility — not to mention delicious taste — of this cooking method.

And you'll also find all of those delicious beef chuck roasts, as well as all-time favorites like chicken casserole with dumplings, collard greens and Simple gingered ribs. We've got slow cooker recipes you and your entire family will love for years to come.

76990045R00058

Made in the USA
Columbia, SC
13 September 2017